Easy to Play Cello Airs and Ballads

Gene Clarke

WWW.MELBAY.COM

Foreword

Many beautiful melodies –both folk songs and "composed" popular songs– originated in Great Britain and the United States during the nineteenth and early twentieth centuries. *Easy to Play Cello Airs and Ballads* is a collection of twenty-five of these tunes arranged in a way that can be enjoyed by student and amateur cellists of all ages.

All the tunes are written entirely in first position, with bowing indications and fingerings for any unusual accidentals marked. Chord names are included for accompaniment by a guitarist or player of any chord-capable instrument. Every song can also be played along with the corresponding title in *Easy to Play Violin Airs and Ballads* and *Easy to Play Viola Airs and Ballads.*

I thank Mr. William Bay for encouraging me to write this book and helping me select the tunes herein. I hope all of you enjoy playing these melodies as much as I have enjoyed collecting, arranging, and playing through them!

Gene Clarke

Contents

Fingerpicking or Strumming

All the Pretty Horses

Traditional Lullaby
arranged by Gene Clarke

Barbara Allen

Traditioinal Scottish Ballad
arranged by Gene Clarke

Bonnie Dundee

Scottish Folk Tune
arranged by Gene Clarke

Botany Bay

Australian Folk Song
arranged by Gene Clarke

In the Days of Forty-Nine

Traditional American Ballad
arranged by Gene Clarke

Steadily-not too fast

George Collins

Old English Ballad
arranged by Gene Clarke

Slowly

Handsome Molly

Traditional Old-Time Song
arranged by Gene Clarke

I Am a Pilgrim

Southern Gospel Tune, 1864
arranged by Gene Clarke

I Ride an Old Paint

Cowboy Song, Early 1900's
arranged by Gene Clarke

In the Good Old Summertime

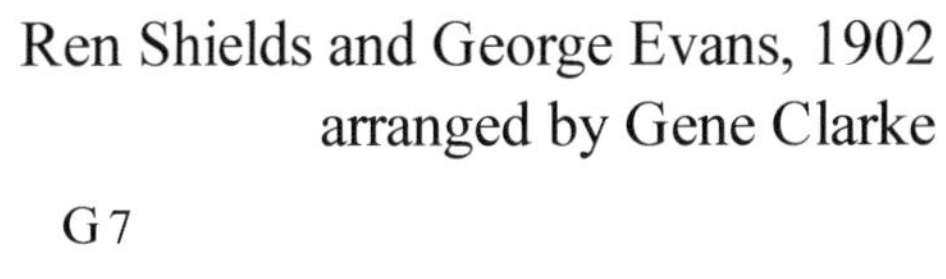

Lilting

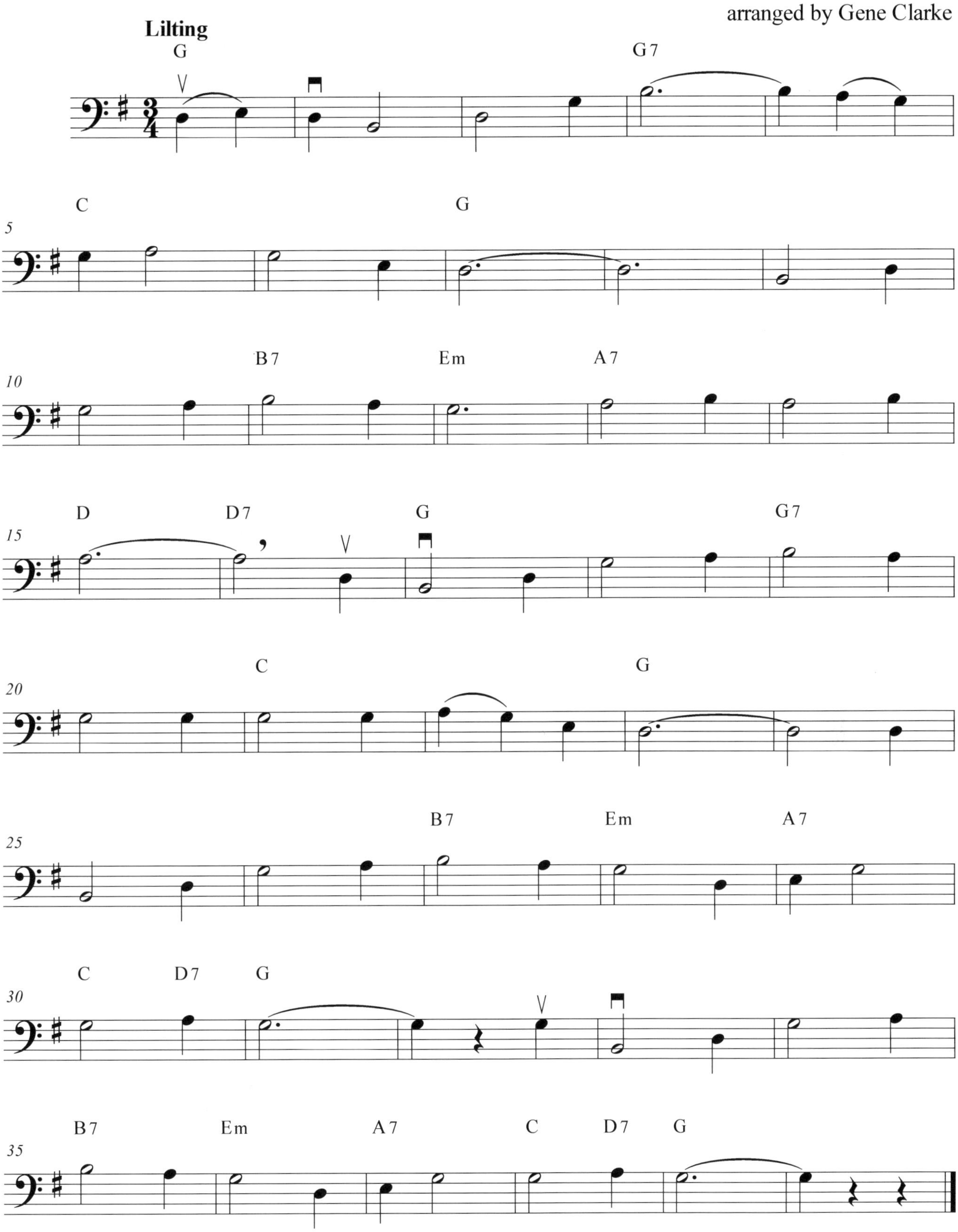

Listen to the Mockingbird

Septimus Winner, 1855
arranged by Gene Clarke

The Little Old Log Cabin in the Woods

William S. Hays,1871
arranged by Gene Clarke

Lynchburg Town

Frank Spencer, 1848
arranged by Gene Clarke

Lively

C G C

6
G C

11
G C F C G

16
C D A

21
D A D

26
A D G D

31
A D G D

35
A D G D

The Old Oaken Bucket

George F. Kiallmark, 1826
arranged by Gene Clarke

Only a Bird in a Gilded Cage

Arthur J. Lamb and Harry von Tilzer, 1900
arranged by Gene Clarke

Over the Garden Wall

Harry Hunter and George D. Fox, 1879
arranged by Gene Clarke

Pretty Saro

Traditional American Tune, Early 1900's
arranged by Gene Clarke

Sweet Polly Oliver

English Broadside Ballad, 1840
arranged by Gene Clarke

The Banks of the Ohio

19th Century Ballad

Arranged by Gene Clarke

The Letter Edged in Black

Hattie Nevada, 1899
arranged by Gene Clarke

The Mermaid's Song

Scottish Air
arranged by Gene Clarke

The Mist-Covered Mountains

Traditional Scottish Air
arranged by Gene Clarke

fingerpicking accomp.

The Parting Glass

Traditional Irish Tune
arranged by Gene Clarke

The Rose of Tralee

19th Century Irish Folk Song
arranged by Gene Clarke

Slow and sentimental

The Wagoner's Lad

Old Time Ballad, 1907
arranged by Gene Clarke

Moving along

D G D G D G A D

5 A D G D A D A

10 D G D A G D G A

15 D A G D G C G C G C

20 D G D G C G

24 D G D G C G

28 D Em D C D G D C

32 G G D C G